The
City Fox

The *City Fox*

and
others
in our community

CHRIS PARKER

urbanepublications.com

First published in Great Britain in 2015
by Urbane Publications Ltd
Suite 3, Brown Europe House,
33/34 Gleamingwood Drive,
Chatham, Kent ME5 8RZ

A CIP catalogue record for this book is available from the
British Library.

ISBN 978-1-909273-45-0
EPUB 978-1-909273-46-7

Cover by Luke Fielding

Text design & typeset by Chandler Design

Printed in Great Britain
by CPI Group (UK) Ltd,
Croydon, CR0 4YY

urbanepublications.com

The publisher supports the Forest Stewardship Council® (FSC®), the leading
international forest-certification organisation. This book is made from acid-free
paper from an FSC®-certified provider. FSC is the only forest-certification scheme
supported by the leading environmental organisations, including Greenpeace.

To Eddie,
Thank you for supporting
- and I hope you enjoy -
the City Fox.
(Lessons in Silat...)
Love
Chris Parkes
April 2015.

'We learn through
community -
even when alone.'

Epiah Khan

Contents

A poet's biography

In a brown, tattered case

As far as I can tell I wrote my first poem in 1966. I was nine years old. I say *as far as I can tell* because it is the first poem in a hand written notebook creatively titled *A Book of Verse* that I wrote between then and 1970. I have no evidence of any earlier attempts to write poetry, so I think this was the beginning.

I would like to believe that my inspiration was England's World Cup win in the summer of that year, but as the poem is actually about Christmas I suspect it was inspired by childish thoughts of the Nativity and Santa Claus and a selfish desire for a sack full of presents.

For a reason I cannot now fathom I recorded the year I wrote each poem. For reasons that are far more obvious I forgot all about the notebook and its contents when I reached puberty. Subsequent notebooks recorded other things. Some of those were significant enough to have the dates put along side them, too.

I found *A Book of Verse* just over two years ago when my mother died and the men in a van came round to empty the family home of all the furniture and ornaments that I had not been able to give to a better cause. The notebook was in an old, brown, tattered case underneath a bed in what we used to call the spare room.

When the men left I sat on the lounge floor and read the work of a child. It's funny how scruffy and disfigured the inside of a house looks, how differently it smells, when the men in a van have ripped its guts out. The work of a child doesn't help your mood in that situation. It doesn't encourage you to leave either. I did, of course. I had to. I had already sold the place to someone who had recognised its investment potential.

I took the notebook away with me. And once again forgot about it. Until today. Until just now. Until I sat down to write what Matthew, my publisher, had asked for. Matthew is a very good man and a very good friend and a very good editor and publisher, and he had said,

'Chris, I need a biography that's more poetry-related than your usual one about education, communication and influence.'

Matthew, this is it. For all my adult life I have been committed to education, in one form or another, and especially to communication and influence. I have, it seems, been a writer for longer. I was, it seems, a poet first. I still am.

Chris
2015.

A poet's foreword

In the city

Many years after I wrote *The Book of Verse* and well before I found it again, I said to my teacher, 'I really respect those people who are so dedicated they leave everything behind to go in search of themselves and their God.'

He replied, 'So do I. However, I respect even more those who do the same thing whilst remaining in the city. You see, in the roar of the city worlds collide. They jar against each other. Connections are hidden behind man-made distractions that seek to fill our minds. It is easy to become lost.'

Then he led me on a walk through busy streets. He didn't speak to me again for more than a year.

My teacher continues to live in the city.

An introduction to The Community

People

Writer, swordsmith, gardener, Mary, Peter, priest, soldier, charity worker, old man, dog walker, grandson, schoolteacher, schoolboy, Martin, newsagent, occasional farm boy, uncle, homeless man sitting on damp cardboard, travellers, business guru, Jean, Syd, neighbours, me, Epiah Khan (possibly).

Places

Home, garden, cloud factory, black-as-coal road, city, waste ground, playing fields, canal-side, bed, supermarket, school, pavement, farm, outside the bank, hospital, pub, city parks, outside the bakery, petrol station.

Nature in the city

Bird, flowers, wind, ice, leaf, bud, seasons,
summer clouds, gardens, hedgerow, bushes,
spaniel, canal, weather, night sky, cat, bee,
worm, dog, the city fox.

Writer

I wake early.
Every home in the street is in darkness,my
wife softened on our bed,
the air in other rooms untouched.
I have no idea of the words,
only a need, overwhelming even sleep, to sit
at this desk,
shadowed by my favourite lamp,
to roll between my fingers the ink pen that
no one else must use.

Desperate, I take a breath meaning to use it
and as I struggle with the inevitable gap
a bird sings in the coldness of the garden.
Just a bird I never see
singing to no one in particular,
singing from its heart
because it has to.

How can a bird do so easily the thing I find
most difficult?
Why is my pen so distant?

Learning language

Bun bu ichi
the Japanese phrase
speaks of the two great powers,
the pen and the sword,
by which we shape our world.

At least the sword
beautiful and balanced
which can kill in less than an instant
is forged in fire,
its edge so sharp it barely exists.

This is pure transformation.

Dullness stretched and cultured
into a tool, a symbol, an artist's gift.
Its creator, drenched in sweat,
honoured for his sacrifice,
keeping hands close to nature,
breath hissing into the flames.

If only our words were crafted in such a way,
could serve such purpose,
reflect such commitment.
Instead our word-swords wound by accident.

- cutting ourselves, you understand, as well
as others - running amok with sound
and shape.

Perhaps one day a sword-smith will teach
children how to shape their words,
brighten their senses,
sharpen their silence.

Gardener

When nature makes a decision
there's no going back.
She keeps her silence,
letting the birds and the flowers
the wind and the ice
speak on her behalf.

When nature makes a decision
She's teaching us.

Gardener (ii)

Nature is no timekeeper.

The leaf doesn't fall when it does because
time is money.
The bud doesn't open to maintain this
week's schedule.
Nature doesn't count the seasons because
they are her.

Nature has no plan.

She left that to us.

Hunter

So when is the beginning?

Does the hunt start when the prey is sensed,
or with the first pangs of hunger?

Or is it further back
at birth
or even before?

Does it begin with a question
or with desire?

Is the hunt
part of the hunter
like a limb or an organ?
Or is it just a behaviour
as necessary as breath?

And when does it end?
Is it with the kill, the feed, or the
transference into energy?

Is our ability to ask these questions
the source of our power
or the cause of our limitation?

Can a hunter have an intellect?

Mary & Peter

They were the best of friends.
The very best.
Since the sacred oath taken on the day when
they were just more than children and
just less than the promise of the morning sun,
- before their first lover and long before
their first loss,
before they began counting time through
the growth of others,
before either knew what it really meant -
they pledged a lifetime of friendship.
The very best.
Even partners said, 'Those two have
no secrets.'

Yet often it would wake him in the night
tugging him from sleep
to wonder in silence how it might have been.

And for all his life he knew the smell of her.

Summer clouds

The cloud factory, standing next to the
black-as-coal road
that twists and winds its way like a frozen river,
spews out grey, venomous clouds that
threaten harm and dampen spirits.

I've heard it said they've closed the factories
that make summer clouds.

Priest

secret notes

When I wake in the morning the first thing
I turn to
in this wondrous world
is
Me.
The things my body needs
the race my mind insists upon
the fears my ego-self creates for the
coming day.

With the answers all around me
I choose instead to go inwards
stopping short of the sacred-place.

Soldier

back from Afghanistan

I'm rushing towards a future of my own
creation, all of it bleak.

What part of me feels the need to ignore the
bright emptiness of the space ahead and see
only darkness?
What part of me returns to this endlessly
when I walk through the city?
Why do I hurt myself?

Today I walked through a thousand lives.
Each as precious as mine.
Perhaps
a woman trembling at the promise of a
new career,
a man praying silently for an ailing friend,
a couple who had just made love,
a mother missing her children for an afternoon,
a teacher light with his sharing.

I didn't see one of them.

I know they didn't see me.

Charity worker

I have never been able to give without
needing something in return.
Most of all I seek the joy of giving
unexpectedly and freely,
of watching it ripple through the mind and
body of another.

Oh, my false-heart!

Researchers say *Because* is a powerful word.
It promises reasons and justifications
offers explanations and understanding.
It is the link between cause and effect.
It is the life-blood of the Scientist.

I understand *Because*.
Sometimes it is part of my disguise.
Sometimes it is my apology.
It is always the reason for my giving.

The God I believe in knows everything apart
from this word.

The city fox

The city fox shares everything she has with
her family.
She teaches by her example how to survive
in the grey forest.

From her the cubs learn how to make any
place their home,
how to avoid distraction.
They learn the value of invisibility,
the power that comes from weakness,
how to live in the shadows.

The darkness is no place for adaptation or
creativity.
Around the waste of human existence there
is no need for imagination or expectation.
In the hedgerow and the garden bushes
the waste ground and the playing fields,
just the keenest nose and the sharpest
hearing bring reward:
another day in hiding
another night to hunt.

The old man

Some people say that the old man at 102 is
a mystic
who retired early to dedicate himself
to prayer.
They say that he speaks in tongues
and dances in his garden to the music of
the angels.

Some people say that the old man is mad
because he is always happy,
even though he knows they have closed the
factories that make summer clouds.

Dog walker

How curious and excited
the spaniel
racing and twisting by the canal
for the second time in the day,
empty and open
joyous
and
timeless.

Trembling
she rushes,
travelling on her breath
every difference a new world.

One
and
one
and
one.

All else forgotten.

Influence

We came into this world
not because we had a plan
but because someone else did.

We came into this world
not through conflict nor seeking it,
knowing only how to play and learn,
how to be grateful,
curious
and brave.

Who taught us to change?

So much we can do in one minute

My grandson is learning the hardest of
things.
Dragging himself upright he takes
faltering steps
towards inevitable collapse;
with tears varnishing his cheeks
he reaches for his mother
his cries dissolving at her touch,
ready in a heartbeat to start again
as if nothing bad had happened.

Soldier (ii)

Sometimes Death touches,
fills me briefly
in my gut and mind
and so many thoughts press
heavy and cold
that I hear none of them.

Where am I?

Sometimes
- these very different times -
Death strokes the fear my mind creates
and I cry at the freedom in its promise.

Who am I?

Mary & Peter (ii)

She spoke with her back turned to him
in the coldness of their bed
in the darkness of their room.

She could not speak of loneliness or fear
not now
when she had to be so precise
not now
with her back turned as a warning sign.
Instead she told him of her anger and
disappointment,
her investment going unrewarded.

With her back serving as a barrier
she looked forward, blinking occasionally,
into the darkness.

Priest (ii)

on counselling

Oh! To be able to see so clearly that we
understand another by reading the lines on
their face,
by watching the movements of their
fingertips,
by the glance of their eyes.
To listen so acutely that we hear the voices
of their past or their fears for the future
through their words in the present.
To be so interested in others that our senses
tingle at every opportunity
to know them better.

Or, instead, to stay imprisoned in our
own body,
warded by our own thoughts?

The old man (ii)

'Why not just give yourself up to the
inevitability of success?'
The old man at 102 spoke to me suddenly as
we queued in our local supermarket.

'Why not just give yourself up to the
inevitability of success
the way a cat
gives herself up
to the stone floor
in the heat
of the summer sun?

'After all, everyone becomes great at
something.
It can be eating, or smoking, or fear.
It can be doubt or denial.
It can be lack of awareness.
So why not make it giving
in all its many forms?
Why not make it joy?
Why not just surrender to the stone?

'Aah! I must stop now.
Look - it's your turn to pay.'

Measurement

'You must do your best,'
the schoolteacher said.

The boy's eyes widened
and because he had not yet been taught
about percentages,
did not yet understand the importance of
exams,
was ignorant of measurements and systems
and instead knew
only
how to be curious
he asked,
'How will I know ever know when I have
done my best?

Schoolteacher

I hurt too easily
when
others
do not behave how I expect them to,
when
the weather
is not as I hoped,
when
results
do not go my way.

Yet
rarely do I meet my own expectations;
rarely am I the person
I believe in.

And still there are people who love me.

Wrapping

My grandson plays with the paper rather
than the gift.
He slaps it with his palms.
He pulls and tumbles backwards.
He tears and scrunches
and oh so quickly favours another piece.

His parents watch, taking photos with their
iPhones,
comfortable and proud,
secure in their new-build,
on hand when the wrapping proves too
much.

Martin

alone

I have made a business of my life,
played my part in creating a city of
expectation.
(Although I show my weakness often by
claiming it the work of others.)

I could have learned from the city fox
comfortable in the shadows,
from the branch bending gladly this way
and that,
from the spaniel forgetful and joyous.

I could have blessed the flower for offering
its delicate face
full to the heavens.
I could have found release in loss,
swopped every agenda for just a little
more awareness.

I could have been led by the seasons and not
by the clock,
thought less about winning and more
about service,

created words on the forge of curiosity and
in the fire of love,
celebrated without an audience
like a bird singing in the chill of the early
morning.

I could have…

Only I was too busy making a business of my
life, you see
and now I fear it is too late;
I am so much the creation of my own habits.

Although - wait! -
I hear the city fox
whispering,
'Human! Listen!
There is always time for rebirth.
This alone is nature's business.
The universe is all around you.
Always.
You are still small enough to grow!'

And I believe her - I have to -
my hope,
the city fox.

Soldier (iii)

I am so trammelled up with fear
I cannot think about what comes next.

I will not meet my final death this way.

Newsagent

closing down

It's snowing
again.
Cold, freezing winds
blowing all the way from the Arctic.
Roads closed.
Train lines down.
The city stilled by the worst winter for
twenty years.

It doesn't matter that they can't walk to me
in this.
Truth is, they don't need to leave their
home.
They don't even need to turn real pages.
They certainly don't need me when news
is 24/7
when everything is only one click away
when we can see everything
show everything
comment on everything
protected by a password and the screen
of entitlement
supported by friends and followers we have
never met

and never will
joined by the frostbite of technology
numbing our senses
blackening our reach.

Truth is, this is how it always ends
closing the door for the last time
one click
empty and quiet.
Frozen.

Pavement clues

The residue of a thought
clings
like snow to a pavement;
sometimes it hardens, thickens,
becoming treacherous;
sometimes it dissolves in unexpected heat.

The residue of a thought
there
beneath our footprint.

Occasional farm boy

lost outside the city

Invest in loss, the sage advised.
Care enough to be curious.
Love enough to risk.
Create hope.

Only that was then and this is now.
Only *plus ça change plus c'est la*
même chose.
Only it cannot have been the same for a
man finding wisdom
walking a continent barefoot.
Only why should planes, trains and brogues
make such a difference?

———————————

There was a time when I was not yet into
double figures
when my uncle left me with strict instructions
to keep hold of both dogs
no matter what.
They tugged after him as he strode
towards the barn where the birth was going
badly wrong.

The dogs, mother and son, looked at me
wildness in their eyes
as my uncle disappeared from view.

They tugged again.

The mother, Sally,
- how crazy that a name should sound
so harmless
and yet the mouth seem so threatening -
the mother, Sally, jumped against me.
I staggered back
almost losing my grip on the leash.

This next time they jumped together
their claws scratching my chest, their spittle
flying into my face.

The fragile command that shook itself free
from my throat
was more a plea for understanding than a
demand for peace.
The mother, the wiser of the two, dropped
low, nipping at my ankles,
as her son tried again to force his face
into mine.

My hand opened,

releasing dogs and shame and fear in the
same split-second.

The dogs raced into the barn.
The shame and fear stayed close,
squeezing out tears
crushing my chest.
The cow bellowed. The dogs barked. The
men's raised voices were filled with anger.

This was the first time my imagination broke
free,
running wild
to create the worst of all possible worlds.

My uncle brought it back under control
ten minutes later
returning from the barn with dogs at heel.
His brogues were muddied
there was blood, too.

'Saved them both,' he said. 'Just.'
He took a long, deep breath. 'Next time,' he
glanced at the dogs who sat immediately.
'Next time, keep hold.
Understand?'

———————————

The sage wrote, 'The only thing between yourself and the universe is your skin. You are closer to freedom than you think.'

Perhaps it was different then?

Writer (ii)

We travelled far from home to find relaxation,
to create distance from something we
define, casually, as the
pressure of the city;
we travelled, I guess, in search of peace.

Of course, we stressed about the selection
of clothes, the timings and the paperwork.
We monitored the weather forecasts and the
travel information.
We took computers, Sat Nav and phones;
packed adaptors so that everything would fit
and be fully charged.

Eventually we found the place with blue sky
and greenery,
mountains, fresh water and a different
language.

After two (or maybe three) days
the queues and delays
- the frequent confusion of travel -
were forgotten.

On the sixth day I read this poem out loud,
I think it was the sixth day
because
I know that I hadn't yet started thinking
about the return journey.
When I finished reading
she said, 'I don't understand it all.
Do you?'

'No,' I replied after some delay, 'I am only
the writer.'

I wished, later, that I had said, 'They are
only words.
I just happened to hear them first.'

I wish, most of all, that I could structure my
thoughts without a constant reference
to myself.
Perhaps then I wouldn't need to travel so far.

Mary & Peter (iii)

And in the night
with her back turned to him
with her change in breathing telling him that
she was far away,
that she was lost in her cold emotion,
he chose to wait
and listen
in silence.

At least he said no words out loud.
He offered no contradiction or promise,
no suggestion of warmth.

How could he reach out to her?
Trapped by his choice to make this life enough,
to accept,
rather than start again.

Newsagent (ii)

on reflection

Everything turns full circle.
That is the headline of my life.

I looked into the mirror this morning and
saw my father looking back.
Not the young, muscular version
but rather the old man
with sag and loss
with jowl and bag
with blurry eyes filmed with images of the
past
the future closer
the question *why?*
long since replaced
by the question
when?

I looked into the mirror this morning
and shaved a man I thought was gone.

The city fox (ii)

answering the question

The fox hunts without distraction as the city
whirls around her,
neon signs flashing characters and invitations
cars racing between gears and lights
urgency, wrapped in design, screaming at
the night sky
turning the city ever-inward.

Yet the fox hunts without distraction.
She has her purpose
given irrepressible priority by her young,
left behind,
her nature
more compelling than any fashion.

Her nose flares and twitches
her eyes penetrate the shades of darkness
her pads trace a line set by only the most
pertinent cues.

She kills silently, teeth piercing skin and
crushing bone without warning or posture
or thought.

She has no conscience.
She never has, and never will, fear
consequence.
There is no separation between what she
does and who she is.

Best then, if to die at all, to be killed by the
city fox.

Bank manager

The man was sitting on a piece of damp
cardboard, legs crossed as if in meditation,
with his back to the wall of the bank,
presenting both a challenge and a plea.
At least that was my perception. I never
thought to ask for his.

'Spare a pound,' he said, as I keyed in my
number.
'Why just a pound?'
'The thing I've learnt,' he said, 'is that
everything begins before it begins and
ends after it ends. Perhaps if I'd learnt that
sooner…'

He knew the price of a bed in the nearest
hostel.
(I asked him as if that had always been my
intention.)
When I gave the money I saw fear in his
eyes.
'Move on,'
I said firmly
as if we had struck a deal.

Gardener (iii)

Silence is born in the moment when night
meets morning
when nature passes from one to the other
when the city fox has disappeared,
before the first bird sings.

It's a silence filled with certainty
that can only be felt when there are no more
questions to be asked
no more possibilities to be explored.

It's the silence that exists beyond division;
when the decision has been made.

The old man (iii)

The old man at 102 has died.

He slipped on the damp grass dancing to
the music of the angels.
He broke his hip
survived the operation
then lost his breath
to
complications.

They say that the old man died with a smile
on his face
as if he had heard the answer to a question
as if he was looking past the grey, venomous
clouds.

They say that he died
knowing that it was part of a process.

I wish I knew.

Writer (iii)

If my pen had a life of its own
would the words run free
celebrating their escape from the shackles
of my mind?

Or would they stumble and shiver,
creeping, huddled across the lines of a page
they have never seen before?

Would I recognise them?

Are they my prisoner
or am I theirs?

If my pen had a life of its own
could it answer this?

Travellers

My friend died on Wednesday at 6am.

In a city thousands of miles away it was
another time altogether.
There, in that same split-second,
other lives ended;
lives I will never know.

If reality exists on this earth
perhaps it is somewhere in the space
between two people;
the emptiness we fill.

Cat

The cat pads instinctively into the spotlight
dissolving down onto the warmth of the
stone;
a silk cloth settling over the curves of the
uneven floor.

Her eyes close in immediate submission
and, at once, everything is hidden
the stillness broken only by her belly,
pulsing gently.

This is not performance
this is life so filled to the brim
there is no space for choice.
She does not need to twist and turn to find
her comfort
she does not wonder if she ought to rest
she has never questioned her identity or her
potential.
She has no options
she can be nothing else;
just a perfect cat
giving
herself
to the Earth.

Breath

Without the cultivation of appropriate
resources
even the greatest plan, the most inspiring
vision, the worthiest intention,
is doomed to failure.
This is what the business guru means when
he says,
'The gap between imagination and success
is crossed only on the bridge of resource.'

It is a bridge, he writes, that becomes both
the symbol and the measure of success.
It is a bridge redefined and rebuilt as
success grows.

'Power,' the guru says, 'Is the ability to
cultivate, combine and direct resource.
Power is far more than money, or networks,
than equipment, staffing or skills,
although these are all a part of it.

Power is the ability to summon and
prioritise, to transform the ordinary into
the extraordinary, to create and manage

momentum as no other can.
Power and the symbols of power are all
resource-dependent.'

So he teaches, through workshops and
seminars, through books and dvds.
People flock to him from across the world.
Even in his own land he is a prophet, a
visionary, who proves his truth through his
own example.

And, because he is a guru of business and
only that,
in all his teaching about power and resource
he never mentions breath.

Not once.

Schoolteacher (ii)

The pub was crowded
Friday-tea-time
standing room only in no-man's land.

The schoolteacher saw me look.
Somehow
even though he was on the other side of the bar
even though he was lost in thought
even though it was only a glance.

Eyes in the back of his head
I thought.
Teacher-vision.

He raised his glass to me
barely
just a syllable of movement
his smile even less.

'I'm tired,' the smile said,
'tired of the responsibility of talking
of the weight of listening
of the endless measurements.
Please don't look at me.
It hurts.'

Travellers (ii)

The bee was full and fat and bold in colour
it's wings a measure of excitement and joy
that
I suspect
I cannot even imagine.

Somehow,
even though she was giving every drop of her
attention to the flower
- or, perhaps, for that very reason -
she spurred a question in my mind,
translated in an instant so that I could
if I chose
be grateful and curious and dip in to its offering,
its far less obvious learning.

And have you ever,
the question asked,
forged a route
rather than simply followed one

do you know how it feels for your
footprints to be the first,
to not know what lies ahead
and yet press on?

The question, *Are you an Explorer?*
is
of course
a question about Education,
that process of discovery and development
far removed from the need for clear endings
and right answers and the rush to raise hands
into the air.

The question, 'Are you an Explorer?' asks
how comfortable you are with not knowing,
how free you are from the prison of
comparison,
how far-reaching is your home?

There are always Explorers walking amongst us
waiting patiently,
like all great destinations,
to be discovered.

Bird

the gardener explains how

There is only one chance to make a
first impression;
that is what the experts teach.

Those experts in communication
who know how to structure and sequence,
combine information and emotion,
demand attention.

In the garden the bird's feathers ruffle against
the early morning chill;
she settles quickly
balancing on the pencil-thin branch.

Here, now, she's drawn to the opportunity of
the new day
the openness
the pure space.
It draws the song from her.

She doesn't see the pen
stilled by her voice,
nor the jealous hand.

Jean

When Jean was eight years old she dreamed
of being a princess.

When she was thirteen
she imagined being a pop star.

When she was sixteen
she prayed she wasn't pregnant.

Now - and Jean would never have guessed
this -
she works in the petrol station
and sometimes she sells condoms.

She makes sense of it all.

Her sleeplessness is not caused by her life,
rather by the fact that she does not know
how to sell dreams
to her daughter.

Wrapping (ii)

'Once,' Jean said
after too many glasses of Pinot Grigio,
after Time had been called without any
sense of invitation or request,
'Once,' Jean said, 'I gave my heart
completely.
Silly me,
I chose the wrong words to go with it.'

Syd

In moments of what we would call clarity,
that he might call 'lamp' or 'zoo'
or any other words his damaged brain
and forceful mouth
combined to construct,
Syd recognised what we might call his
irreversible loss,
his change,
his irreparable damage.

In moments of what we would call clarity,
he tried to kill himself.
Those moments stretched by his
determination.

The neighbours and the shopkeepers who
knew him before the stroke
did their best to accommodate him.
'It's such a shame,' they said.
'He was so lovely.'

Towards the end
he wore shorts
even when the weather bit,
his legs stick thin
the muscles wasted.

We never said that his mind and emotion
– to be more precise, his emotional control –
were wasted,
we never said that.
We were more like the neighbours and the
others,
more likely to say how sorry we were
without ever having the courage to consider
who we felt most sorry for.

I doubt we had more moments of clarity
than he.

The second stroke took him like a tidal wave;
washed everything away but the shell.

At his funeral I performed the words I had
written and practised.
I did a good job, they said.
It seemed to help.

Me

I have more skin now than when I began,
but the wrinkles are returning
along with the excess.

My friends say, kindly, that my skin has
character;
a face showing a life lived.
I know only how difficult it is to write a new
story
on a crumpled sheet.

On the day my father died,
asleep,
his skin became unexpectedly smooth;
creases that had been deepening
disappeared below the surface;
a warm pink glazed his cheeks.

If you have ever seen the sun setting
-drifting colours from beyond the horizon-
above a calm sea that was violent only
hours before,
you will know exactly what I mean.

Sometimes I feel comfortable within my skin.
Sometimes I am removed from it, as if
distanced by a lens.
Sometimes I look at the heavens,
feel my heels balanced on the spinning
earth,
and something I cannot quite remember
makes me smile.

E.K?

I met Epiah Khan yesterday outside the bakery.
At least, that was how he introduced himself
as if he knew his name would mean something.

'Man decorates the world', he said without
preamble,
'Man decorates the world through the strength
of his will and the flatulence of his ego.
Remember, knowing is not the same as being.'

Then he offered me a doughnut.

Sam's lesson

I had a dog, Sam,
a squat, red, cheerful fellow
with a wide, easy grin that stretched forever
across muscular cheeks.

He growled at me once, as a young adult still
testing his place,
his head low over his food,
his tongue flicking out, curling over exposed
teeth as if tasting the air between us.

Fortunately this was so unexpected I had no
time to think
- it was the lesson he taught me about instinct
buried just below the surface.

My hands turned him
one swift precise motion onto his back
cupping the underside of his jaw
exposing the softness of his throat
lowering my face over him.

We stayed that way for some time,

seconds stretching into a lifelong understanding.

Often, after that, whenever he felt the need to
press me for affection
he would roll over demanding his belly to
be rubbed,
sharing the pulse in his throat without hesitation.

I found it all but impossible to resist.

Always, after that, I have hugged my friends
clear in the realisation that we place our open
throats against each other's collar;
a sign of trust more significant than the brief
touch of hands or even lips on skin.

Once, after that, I met a woman who closed
the gap so completely
I offered her my throat without question
or doubt.

She took it.

Then offered me her own.

Bird (ii)

The city parks are filled with
people passing through.

Some
listening to music as they run,
planning their day
thoughts faster than their feet.

Those already dressed for work
are slower
no less deliberate
a phone pressed to their ear like a baby to
the breast.

Lovers are the slowest,
hips pressing as they walk
talking through open-mouthed smiles
of shared intimacy
pupils dilated by remembering, imagining
and hope.

In the garden
bird plunges her beak into the soil,
stabbing down without hesitation.

Withdrawing
her head cocks from side to side
- how stupid to think she is listening!

She stabs again
a staccato attack.

Seconds later
look
– there! –
a worm
disturbed
by her effort.

Bird holds her place in triumph,
having shaken the earth.

The old man (iv)

They say
that the old man at 102
left a will.
Not that he had any possessions to pass on
nor anyone who knew him
for that matter.

They say
that in his will
the old man wrote,
'I leave you the grass in my garden.
I hope that one day you are drawn to dance
barefoot in the early morning
when the grass is still damp from the
night's touch,
when the earth is fertile with the new dawn
still as a mother feeding her young.

I pray that you dance from your heart,
that the earth clings to the soles of your feet.
I pray that you search for the silence behind
the noise.'

Martin (ii)

connected

For many years I sought control. Which, of
course, is another way of saying I believed I
had the power to create certainty.
(In my defence it is a common illness.)
I wrote and exercised plans. I developed
resources. I did everything I could to
shape today and tomorrow. Which took all
of my attention.

So I missed the lessons offered to me,
the branch dancing this way and that on
the wind
the flower's face opening to the heavens,
capable only of receiving,
the city fox, slinking, sleeping close by, never
dreaming of the wild forest
nor missing it.

A wise man saw me once in a dream and said,
'Imagine being a circle with a dot at its centre.
A dot you can barely see and yet a circle, too.
Imagine that is your Self.'

This is how he broke me.

'There is a light', he said, 'that can only be lit
by weakness.
It can light a thousand others and is never
diminished by its giving.
It can be a touch, a look, or just a word.'

Once, thank God, as I stood crying
the night sky whispered,
'Nature knows nothing of weakness nor
death, of winning nor losing.'
As the circle opened – just a glimmer I
suspect –
my thoughts dissolved
all knowledge and questions forgotten,
all sense of self lost in that great unknowing.
There, in that timeless place beyond
separation,
I was the city fox.
And all the rest.

Network

Network is just another word for association
which, in turn,
is just another word for connection
and connections flow into each other
leaving us compelled to create meaning
which is, it seems, part of our nature,
whether that is the so-called nature of our
own creation
or that which precedes and surrounds us
and asks nothing more than we learn how
to look.

My career teachers,
whom I called *parent*
knew nothing of this.
Instead of a net working to connect,
combine and create
they saw instead a ladder
steep
with steps beyond the reach of their
imagination
and therefore of my possibility.

Career is just another word for life
or so it seems for many people
and life is just another word for opportunity,
which is the result of space and curiosity
acknowledged and combined to a greater or
lesser degree.

And that great space cries out for teachers
who cast their net towards it,
freed from the need for legacy
or the well of justification,
teachers with nothing to prove
other than their willingness to release
and their strength to support.

And network is,
of course,
a word we use too often
too small
because here
- right now -
in this instant
we are all sharing the world together.

This is our time.

Community centre

One day a city fox braved the edges of the
petrol station.
Jean saw him first, in a quiet moment.

He returned the next day.

She named him Basil.
She told her regulars.
They fed him.
The fox became a regular too.
The cycle was established.

People talked.

People
all sorts of people
shared their particular story of the city fox
who came to be fed
at the petrol station.

People
all sorts of people
came to the petrol station in the hope of
seeing him
or
feeding him.

Sometimes they did.

He disappeared abruptly
presumed dead.

And still they talked.
Even more so, truth be told.
After all, the space needs to be filled.

Beyond the stories, he left his lesson. Which
is simply this:
It takes only one city fox to create a
community.

Or just something else.

Basil

Waiting for everyone to arrive. Oct 1997

His last appearance. Nov 1999

Pictures copyright Michael Ogle, and reproduced
with his kind permission.

The cover image for The City Fox is reproduced with the kind permission of artist **Racheal Bamford**.

Based in Otley, West Yorkshire, Racheal is a full time Architectural Technician, but also excels in two vastly different pursuits; athletics and art!

Racheal has represented GB and England over cross country, road and track. Her proudest moment was competing for England over the steeplechase at the 2014 Commonwealth Games in Glasgow where she finished 7th in a lifetime best time of 9mins 45secs. This ranks her as the 6th fastest ever GB athlete over the 'chase.

While she is away competing, or just as a way to relax at home, Racheal uses her architectural skills to draw animals and landscapes. Her favourite medium is watercolour overlaid with rotring pen. Having studied architecture at university she was drawn back into creating art when her fiancée Zack opened an art gallery in 2013. Since then Racheal has become a full time exhibitor, creating originals and prints unique to The Old Grammar School Gallery, Otley. She is inspired by her much loved house rabbits Muffin and Binky.

Urbane Publications is dedicated to developing new author voices, and publishing fiction, non-fiction & verse that challenges, thrills and fascinates. From page-turning novels to innovative reference books, our goal is to publish what YOU want to read.

Find out more at
urbanepublications.com

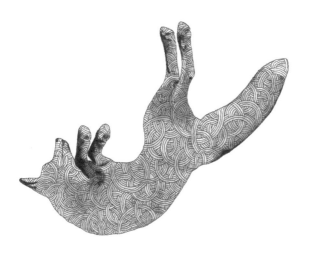